I KEEP MY AFFECTION
IN THE CLOSET

If I were to come back to earth, I'd like to come back as a pillow

JIM DAVIS

A DIET IS TOO LITTLE OF A GOOD THING

JIM DAVIS

Take this jog and shove it

JIM DAVIS

GARFIELD © 1978 United Feature Syndicate, Inc.

© 1983 United Feature Syndicate, Inc.

Monday moves in a mysterious way

JiM DAViS

Diets are for people who want to belittle themselves

GARFIELD

JiM DAViS

I LOVE TO COURT DANGER

JIM DAVIS

11-13

We must all learn to laugh at ourselves

JIM DAVIS

Ever have a day when your timing was off?

JiM DAViS

WHEN IT COMES TO EATING, I'M A GENIUS

JIM DAVIS

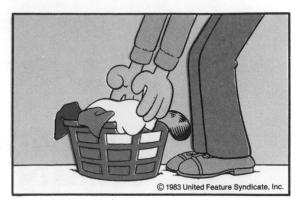

If you want to look thinner... hang around people fatter than you

JIM DAVIS

JIM DAVIS

GARFIELD EATING TIPS

1. Never eat anything that's on fire.

2. Never leave your food dish under a bird cage.

3. Only play in your food if you've already eaten your toys.

4. Eat every meal as though it were your last.

5. Only snack between meals.

6. Chew your food at least once.

7. Avoid fruits and nuts: after all, you are what you eat.

8. Always dress up your leftovers: one clever way is with top hats and canes.

9. A handy breakfast tip: always check your Grape Nuts for squirrels.

10. Don't save your dessert for last. Eat it first.

be your own best friend

JIM DAVIS

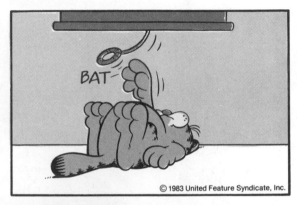

Being a superstar isn't a pretty job but someone has to do it

JiM DAViS

TEDDY BEARS: They don't eat your food, dance with your date, or trump your ace lead.

JIM DAVIS

This business of sleeping holds a great deal of fascination for me

JIM DAVIS

TELL IT TO YOUR PLANTS

JIM DAVIS

JIM DAVIS

GARFIELD: © 1978 United Feature Syndicate, Inc.

SHOW ME A JOGGER AND I'LL SHOW YOU A STRANGE PERSON WITH A THING FOR PAIN

JIM DAViS

Here's to weekends

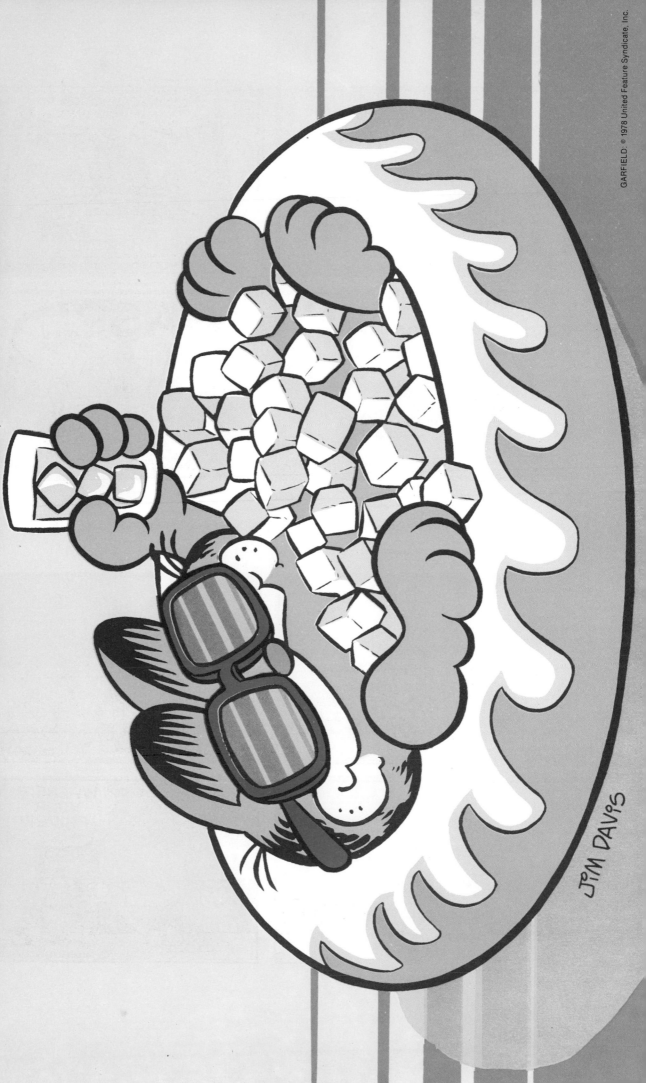

JIM DAVIS

JIM DAVIS

HAVE A NICE DAY

JIM DAVIS

Seasons Greetings

MY ADDRESS HAS CHANGED

GARFIELD: © 1978 United Feature Syndicate, Inc.

Having a wonderful time!

GARFIELD Characters: © 1978 United Feature Syndicate, Inc.

Happy Birthday!

Let me be the first to remind you that you're getting older.

JIM DAVIS

It's your birthday.

JIM DAVIS

Big, fat, hairy deal.